52
Arrival
Activities
for
Children's
Choir

Ginger G. Wyrick

ABINGDON PRESS
Nashville

Contents

52 Arrival Activities for Children's Choir

Copyright © 1999 by Abingdon Press

This book is printed on acid-free, recycled paper.

ISBN 0-687-07313-8

ISBN 13: 978-0-687-07313-9

07 08 09 10 – 10 9 8 7 6 5

MANUFACTURED IN THE UNITED STATES OF AMERICA

Preface

The arrival of children to a rehearsal is an exciting beginning to your time together. The manner in which you choose to greet each child will set the tone for the remainder of the rehearsal. A smile, a hug, addressing each child by name can let a choir member know that he or she is welcome and has a place of worth in your mind. After all, you just took time to acknowledge their presence.

Preparation and organization can ease the transition from the choir room door to the actual rehearsal, especially for those children who arrive early and need to have an activity to occupy a few extra minutes, as well as enhance biblical and musical concepts. Set aside a special place in the choir room for these activities. Let the children know that an activity will always be waiting on them when they arrive at choir. Copy the worksheets in advance and place worksheets and any supplies in this space prior to the rehearsal. If needed, ask an adult volunteer to be present to oversee the activity and provide assistance as needed, especially when working with younger elementary age children.

This collection of activities is designed to provide the director with creative solutions to those minutes before rehearsal. The book is arranged in order of difficulty and concepts are listed for each activity. You may pick and choose which activities to offer to your group based on age appropriateness, concept, and church season. Each page may be duplicated as needed for your choir members.

1. SAME AND DIFFERENT

Age:	Younger Elementary
Concept:	Same and different
Use:	Musical form and note movement
Materials:	Pencils and/or crayons, colored pencils or markers, worksheet #1 (p. 13)

Instructions: This activity is designed for recognition of same and different in preparation for musical form as well as staff reading (note relationships). Have the children circle the pairs that are the same and color the pairs that are different.

Expanded Activity: Look around the rehearsal room for things that look like each other (e.g., two choir robes). Use same and different in your rehearsal such as section A and section B of a song. Use same and different with melodic movement such as repeated notes and notes that move on the staff.

2. BETHLEHEM MAZE

Age:	Younger Elementary
Concept:	Mary and Joseph's journey to Bethlehem
Use:	Advent
Materials:	Pencils and/or crayons, colored pencils or markers, worksheet #2 (p. 14)

Instructions: Complete the maze, then color the picture.

Expanded Activity: Read Luke 2:1-7 with the children. Lead the children in a discussion of the journey to Bethlehem. Ask questions such as "How do you think Mary felt riding that far on a donkey?" "Do you think Joseph got tired walking that far?"

3. MUSIC SYMBOLS SEARCH

Age:	Elementary
Concept:	Music symbol identification
Use:	General review of music symbols
Materials:	Pencils and/or crayons, colored pencils or markers, worksheet #3 (p. 15)

Instructions: Locate and circle each hidden musical symbol; color the picture.

Expanded Activity: Locate these and other symbols in the music you are currently rehearsing. Define each term and have the children demonstrate the concept in a "creative" manner.

Hidden Terms: *D.C., D.S., a tempo, fine, dim., rit.,* **mp, p, mf**

Hidden Symbols: First ending, second ending, fermata, crescendo, diminuendo, segno

4. CODED PICTURE

Age:	Younger Elementary
Concept:	Music symbol identification
Use:	Christmas, general review of music symbols
Materials:	Pencils and/or crayons, colored pencils or markers, worksheet #4 (p. 16)

Instructions: Color the picture using the code.

Expanded Activity: Read Luke 2:8-20 with the children. Lead the children in a discussion of the birth of Christ.

5. COSMIC WORKSHEET

Age:	Younger Elementary
Concept:	Line and space notes
Use:	Identification of line and space notes
Materials:	Pencils and/or crayons, colored pencils or markers, worksheet #5 (p. 17)

Instructions: Draw a line from each spaceship to its correct landing port: Space notes dock at the space station and line notes dock at the line station. Color the picture.

Expanded Activity: Identify line and space notes in the music you are currently rehearsing. Talk about how notes move on the staff (up and down) and demonstrate how the sound changes (high and low).

6. INSTRUMENT MAZE

Age:	Elementary
Concept:	Psalm 150
Use:	General activity on praising God
Materials:	Pencils and/or crayons, colored pencils or markers, worksheet #6 (p. 18)

Instructions: Help the instruments praise God. Find a path for each instrument to God. Color the picture.

Expanded Activity: Discuss other ways we can offer praise to God.

7. A MUSICAL CHECKLIST

Age:	Elementary
Concept:	Music in my life
Use:	General activity on music awareness
Materials:	Pencils, worksheet #7 (p. 19)

Instructions: See how many different ways you use music. Put an X in the box next to the ways you have used music.

Expanded Activity: Take a poll of the choir members to compare how music is used. Make a list of everyone who takes lessons for future instrumental parts in anthems. This activity may be paired with "Music at My Church" (#8).

8. MUSIC AT MY CHURCH

Age:	Elementary
Concept:	Music leadership
Use:	General activity on musicians in my church
Materials:	Pencils, worksheet #8 (p. 20)

Instructions: Discover the music leaders in your church. Answer each question by writing your answer in the blank.
Expanded Activity: Invite various music leaders to attend your rehearsal throughout the year. This will allow the children to meet these people and get to know more about their jobs in the church. This activity may be paired with "A Musical Checklist" (#7).

9. TIME FOR GETTING ACQUAINTED

Age:	Elementary
Concept:	Building community
Use:	First rehearsal icebreaker
Materials:	Pencils, worksheet #9 (p. 21)

Instructions: Have the children ask these questions of each other like a "choir member" scavenger hunt. Once they locate another choir member who fits the question, have that person sign their sheet. The children will meet other choir members and collect autographs at the same time.
Expanded Activity: Have the children share their answers with the entire group. Find out how many different people fit each question (e.g., three people have an older brother).

10. BALLOON RHYTHM WORKSHEET

Age:	Younger Elementary
Concept:	Rhythm (quarter and eighth notes)
Use:	Rhythm identification
Materials:	Pencils and/or crayons, colored pencils or markers, worksheet #10 (p. 22)

Instructions: Connect each child to the balloon that matches the shirt. Color the picture.
Expanded Activity: Create each rhythm by tapping the pattern or playing on a percussion instrument. Next, have an adult point to the balloons in random order as the children tap or play the various patterns.

11. RHYTHMIC LANGUAGE WORKSHEET

Age:	Elementary
Concept:	Rhythm—long and short (quarter and eighth notes)
Use:	Reinforce rhythm
Materials:	Pencils, worksheet #11 (p. 23)

Instructions: Identify each note value as either long or short. Write the appropriate letter below each symbol.
Expanded Activity: Speak the patterns using the rhythmic language. Clap the patterns. Have unpitched rhythm instruments available, and have the children play the patterns on the instruments.

12. MELODIC MOVEMENT GAME

Age:	Younger Elementary
Concept:	Melodic movement
Use:	Introduce how notes move on the staff
Materials:	Pencils, worksheet #12 (p. 24)

Instructions: These traveling notes are moving all around the staff. The children are to write two items: how the note moves horizontally (step, skip, or repeat), and how the note moves vertically (up or down).
Expanded Activity: Identify melodic movement in music you are currently rehearsing. Help the children recognize steps, skips, and repeated notes as well as pitch direction. If you have older children or adult helpers, you may combine this activity with "For the Beauty of the Earth" Scale Step Worksheet (#29).

13. WHERE IS MY THIRD?

Age:	Elementary
Concept:	Interval Study (5-3)
Use:	Follow-up concept review on intervals (5-3)
Materials:	Pencils, worksheet #13 (p. 25)

Instructions: Children are to write the corresponding third scale tone based on the fifth scale tone printed on the page. Help the children notice that a line 5 moves to a line 3 and a space 5 moves to a space 3.
Expanded Activity: Place a barred instrument and mallets in the arrival activities area. Have an adult play a pitch on the instrument to represent the fifth; ask the child to play the third. Also, locate examples of the 5-3 pattern in the music you are currently rehearsing. This activity may be combined with the 5-3-1 Worksheet (#30).

14. PSALM 23 WORD SEARCH

Age:	Elementary
Concept:	Psalm 23
Use:	Lent; study of Psalm 23
Materials:	Pencils, worksheet #14 (p. 26)

Instructions: Find these words in the sheep.
Expanded Activity: Read Psalm 23 with the children. Lead the children in a discussion of this psalm, including the concept of God as a shepherd. Sing a song or anthem based on this scripture. Challenge the children to memorize this psalm.

15. ADVENT HIDDEN WORD PUZZLE

Age:	Elementary
Concept:	Words associated with Advent
Use:	Advent
Materials:	White 8 1/2" x 11" paper, pencils, colored pencils, crayons or markers, worksheet #15 (p. 27)

Instructions: Locate and circle the hidden words from the word list.
Expanded Activity: Have white 8 1/2" x 11" paper and colored pencils, crayons, or markers available. Ask the children to select one word from the word search and draw a picture to show its use during Advent.

16. CHRISTMAS WORD SEARCH

Age:	Elementary
Concept:	Words associated with Christmas
Use:	Christmas
Materials:	Butcher paper or newsprint, colored pencils, crayons or markers, pencils, worksheet #16 (p. 28)

Instructions: Locate and circle the hidden words from the word list.
Expanded Activity: Create a Christmas mural. Have a long sheet of butcher paper or newsprint available with colored pencils, crayons, or markers. Ask the children to create a mural to represent the Christmas story. Display the mural in the choir room or in the hall just outside the room.

17. I SING A SONG OF THE SAINTS OF GOD

Age:	Elementary
Concept:	Hymn study
Use:	All Saints Day; follow-up study of "I Sing a Song of the Saints of God"
Materials:	Pencils, worksheet #17 (p. 29)

Instructions: Fill in the missing words from this hymn using the words printed on the worksheet.
Expanded Activity: Sing this hymn using the completed worksheet. For a special challenge, distribute the blank worksheet and use as a "word chart" to assist the children in memorizing this text. This activity may be combined with the Hymn Page Worksheet (#19) or the Saints Hidden Message (#28).

18. ONCE IN ROYAL DAVID'S CITY

Age:	Elementary
Concept:	Hymn study
Use:	Christmas
Materials:	Pencils and/or crayons, colored pencils, or markers, worksheet #18 (p. 30)

Instructions: Fill in the missing words from this hymn using the words printed on the worksheet. Color the picture.
Expanded Activity: Sing this hymn using the completed worksheet. For a special challenge, distribute the blank worksheet and use as a "word chart" to assist the children in memorizing this text. This activity may be combined with the Hymn Page Worksheet.

19. HYMN PAGE WORKSHEET

Age:	Elementary
Concept:	Hymn study
Use:	Identify information on a hymn page; combine with hymn word search as expanded activity or use as a follow-up activity the next week
Materials:	Pencils, hymnal, worksheet #19 (p. 31)

Instructions: Duplicate one sheet to use as your master. Based on the hymn you are to study, write the name of the hymn on the hymn title line. Duplicate this sheet for each choir member.
Expanded Activity: Sing the hymn. Use the hymn index to locate other hymns that have the same composer, author, hymn tune, meter, or subject.

20. MY HYMNAL WORKSHEET

Age:	Elementary
Concept:	Hymnal study
Use:	Hymnal resources
Materials:	Pencils, hymnal, worksheet #20 (p. 32)

Instructions: This sheet may be used as a review or an introduction to the resources in your hymnal. Be sure your children know how to locate the indexes, worship aides, and hymn pages before giving this as an arrival activity.
Expanded Activity: May be used with My #1 Choice Worksheet (#21).

21. MY #1 CHOICE

Age:	Elementary
Concept:	Hymn study
Use:	Follow-up to study of the hymnal
Materials:	Pencils, hymnal, worksheet #21 (p. 33)

Instructions: Give each child a hymnal. Have the child locate his or her favorite hymn and complete the worksheet.
Expanded Activity: Have the choir sing one stanza of each member's favorite hymn. Make a list of favorite hymns of the choir and display in the choir room. May be used with My Hymnal Worksheet (#20).

22. "COME, CHRISTIANS, JOIN TO SING!" WORD SEARCH

Age:	Elementary
Concept:	Hymn study
Use:	Follow-up to study of "Come Christians, Join to Sing"
Materials:	Pencils, worksheet #22 (p. 34)

Instructions: Locate and circle the hidden words from the word list.
Expanded Activity: Sing this hymn. This activity may be combined with the Hymn Page Worksheet (#19).

23. THE BEATITUDES MATCHING ACTIVITY

Age:	Elementary
Concept:	Beatitudes
Use:	Study of the Beatitudes
Materials:	Pencils, Bible, worksheet #23 (p. 35)

Instructions: Locate Matthew 5:1-11 in the Bible. Match each item on the left with a phrase on the right.
Expanded Activity: Read Matthew 5:1-11. Have the children create a list a persons or situations that fit each item in the left column. Let the children share their responses with the group. Ask why each person or situation was included.

24. THINGS WE DO IN CHOIR

Age:	Elementary
Concept:	Music symbol review and choir awareness
Use:	Early in the choir year
Materials:	Pencils, worksheet #24 (p. 36)

Instructions: Use the symbols to decode the hidden message.
Expanded Activity: Review each symbol including its name and what it does. Have the children add to the list of "things we do in choir."

25. RHYTHM SKELETON

Age:	Elementary
Concept:	Rhythm; hymn study of "Now Thank We All Our God"; fermata
Use:	Introduction or follow-up on the study of "Now Thank We All Our God"
Materials:	Pencils, worksheet #25 (p. 37)

Instructions: Write the rhythmic language in the blanks provided. Clap and speak each pattern. Be sure your choir is familiar with the fermata before using this activity.
Expanded Activity: Have non-pitched percussion instruments in the activity area. Invite the children to play the rhythm patterns once they have completed the worksheet. Challenge the children to identify this mystery hymn. You may choose to follow this by singing "Now Thank We All Our God." Note the similar patterns in lines 1-2 and also in lines 3-4. This activity may be combined with the Hymn Page Worksheet (#19).

26. SEPTEMBER: A FUN TIME OF YEAR

Age:	Elementary
Concept:	Rhythm
Use:	Early fall; review rhythms (quarter, eighth, and quarter rest)
Materials:	Worksheet #26 (p. 38)

Instructions: Identify the rhythm in example 1. Clap and speak each pattern using rhythmic language. Speak the rhythm using the words printed on the worksheet. Repeat for each set. Perform the entire worksheet as a round.
Expanded Activity: Have percussion instruments in the activity area. Once the worksheet is complete, children may play each pattern on an instrument. Have various instruments accompany the voices as they speak the round. Look for these and other rhythms in the music you are currently rehearsing.

27. SCRIPTURE MATCH: "WERE YOU THERE"

Age:	Older Elementary
Concept:	Hymn study with scripture references; note identification
Use:	Holy Week; follow-up study for "Were You There"
Materials:	Pencils, hymnal, Bible, worksheet #27 (p. 39)

Instructions: Look up each scripture reference and draw a line to the appropriate phrase from "Were You There." Circle the notes from the scale that are used in the hymn.
Expanded Activity: Sing this hymn. This activity may be

combined with the Hymn Page Worksheet (#19). Lead the children in a discussion of the Crucifixion.

28. SAINTS HIDDEN MESSAGE

Age:	Older Elementary
Concept:	Hymn study with "I Sing a Song of the Saints of God"
Use:	All Saints Day; follow-up to study of "I Sing a Song of the Saints of God"
Materials:	Pencils, worksheet #28 (p. 40)

Instructions: Use the secret code to fill in each blank. Write the shaded letters in the boxes provided, then unscramble to discover who these people are.

Expanded Activity: Locate these people in the hymn "I Sing a Song of the Saints of God." Sing this hymn. This activity may be combined with the "I Sing a Song of the Saints of God" Fill-in-the-Blank Worksheet (#17).

29. "FOR THE BEAUTY OF THE EARTH" SCALE STEP WORKSHEET

Age:	Elementary
Concept:	Melodic movement; hymn study
Use:	Fall/Thanksgiving; follow-up to melodic movement study; combine with study of the hymn "For the Beauty of the Earth"
Materials:	Pencils, worksheet #29 (p. 41)

Instructions: Look at each shaded area. Identify the melodic movement. In the upper blank, tell if the notes move up, down, or remain the same. In the lower blank, tell if the notes move by step, skip, or repeat.

Expanded Activity: Sing this hymn. This activity may be combined with the melodic movement game. Identify melodic movement in songs or anthems you are currently rehearsing.

30. 5-3-1 WORKSHEET

Age:	Elementary
Concept:	Interval study 5-3-1
Use:	Follow-up concept review on intervals 5-3-1
Materials:	Pencils, worksheet #30 (p. 42)

Instructions: Children are to write the corresponding third and first scale tones based on the fifth scale tone printed on the page. Show the children that a line 5 moves to a line 3 and a line 1. A space 5 moves to a space 3 and a space 1.

Expanded Activity: Place a barred instrument and mallets in the arrival activities area. Have an adult play a pitch on the instrument to represent the 5; ask the child to play the third and first. Also, locate examples of the 5-3-1 pattern in the music you are currently rehearsing. This activity may be combined with the "Where Is My Third?" Worksheet (#13).

31. ANTHEM CLUES

Age:	Elementary (younger children will need assistance)
Concept:	Musical instructions and form within a song or anthem
Use:	With any song to focus on dynamics and tempo
Materials:	Pencils and music to study (song or anthem), worksheet #31 (p. 43)

Instructions: The intent of this activity is to focus the child on the specific musical instructions and form of a given song or anthem. Give each child a copy of a song or anthem you are currently rehearsing. Complete the questions based on that piece. This activity may be repeated with each new piece.

Expanded Activity: Discuss the answers and locate the responses in the music. Sing the song or anthem incorporating these musical instructions.

32. TEST YOUR SKILLS

Age:	Elementary
Concept:	Music symbols and terms review
Use:	Apply this worksheet to any song, hymn, or anthem you are currently rehearsing that has the measure numbers marked. The children should be familiar with time and key signatures, rhythm, tempo, and dynamics before using this activity.
Materials:	Pencils and copies of the song, hymn, or anthem, worksheet #32 (p. 44)

Instructions: Use your music to find the answers. Write down the measure numbers where you have found the answer.

Expanded Activity: Discuss the answers and locate the responses in the music (such as page number, measure number). Sing the song or anthem incorporating these musical instructions.

33. I'M GETTING LONGER!

Age:	Elementary
Concept:	Rhythm and augmentation
Use:	Review note values and doubling of note values/augmentation
Materials:	Pencils, worksheet #33 (p. 45)

Instructions: Write the rhythm that is twice the value of the given note in the blank. Clap and count each example.
Expanded Activity: Have percussion instruments available in the activity area. Let the children play each rhythm pattern on an instrument as they count. Look for examples of augmentation in the music you are currently rehearsing.

34. INTERVAL CONCENTRATION GAME

Age:	Elementary
Concept:	Interval and pitch recognition
Use:	Combine with interval study, notes on the staff, and/or pitch movement
Materials:	Pencils, worksheet #34 (p. 46)

Instructions: Duplicate the page on different colors of paper. Laminate to strengthen the game cards, then cut them apart. Make one copy (game set) per small group. Turn all the cards face down side by side. The first child turns over a card of choice and another card. If the cards match, the child takes the cards. If not, the cards are turned face down and the next player has a turn. The object is to remember where cards are lying and to match all cards.
Expanded Activity: Sing each card using the scale degree numbers. For older students, identify the note names based on either the treble or bass clef. Locate examples of these interval patterns in the music you are currently rehearsing.

35. RHYTHM ADVENTURE

Age:	Elementary
Concept:	Rhythm
Use:	Rhythmic language review
Materials:	Pencils, worksheet #35 (p. 47)

Instructions: Write the rhythmic language in the blank provided. Clap and speak each pattern.
Expanded Activity: Have various percussion instruments in the activity area. Invite children to play the various patterns once the worksheet is complete. Challenge children to play each pattern in succession until the entire page is played. Locate these and other rhythms in the music you are currently rehearsing.

36. RHYTHM REVIEW

Age:	Elementary
Concept:	Rhythms and rhythmic language
Use:	Review of rhythms and writing rhythmic symbols
Materials:	Pencils, worksheet #36 (p. 48)

Instructions: Fill in the blanks with the correct notes or rests to create rhythm patterns.

Expanded Activity: Speak each rhythm pattern. Clap or tap each rhythm pattern. Have non-pitched percussion instruments in the activity area. Invite the children to play each pattern. Have an adult randomly point to the patterns with the children playing or clapping in response.

37. TEN COMMANDMENTS OF SINGING

Age:	Elementary
Concept:	Good singing habits
Use:	Early in the choir year
Materials:	Pencils, worksheet #37 (p. 49)

Instructions: Add commandments 7 through 10 regarding good habits for singing. Share each person's ideas with the group. Create a chart to reflect their ideas. Display the chart in the choir room as a reminder.
Expanded Activity: Read Exodus 20:1-17. Lead the children in a discussion of Moses and the Ten Commandments. Follow this by challenging the children to memorize the Ten Commandments. Create a contest to see how many can memorize this passage. Consider creating teams to work on this activity, such as division by school grade, or boys against girls. Set a final date and keep a chart displayed in the choir room as a reminder of everyone's progress.

38. MY FAVORITE HYMNS

Age:	Elementary
Concept:	Music in worship; hymn review
Use:	Familiarity with music in worship; parts of worship; use of hymnal
Materials:	Pencils and hymnals, worksheet #38 (p. 50)

Instructions: Select two hymns appropriate for each element of worship. Use the topic index and first line index to assist in locating each hymn. Write the responses in the blanks provided.
Expanded Activity: Take a recent bulletin and circle every use of music in the worship service. Discuss how this music supported the service.

39. CRACK THE CODE! TEXT DECODER

Age:	Elementary
Concept:	God's love for children
Use:	Study of the tune, ST. ANTHONY'S CHORALE with this text
Materials:	Pencils, worksheet #39 (p. 51)

We, Your Children, Praise You

WORDS: Lois Horton Young
MUSIC: Franz Joseph Haydn
Words © 1981 Graded Press; arr. © 1967 Graded Press

Instructions: Decode each line of the text using the chart provided.

Expanded Activity: Teach the song, "We, Your Children, Praise You," which is included in this book. You may also find this tune in your hymnal using the text "We, Thy People, Praise Thee." If your hymnal contains this hymn, teach it in conjunction with this activity.

40. SINGER'S RULES

Age:	Older Elementary
Concept:	Choir habits
Use:	Prior to appearance in worship
Materials:	Pencils, worksheet #40 (p. 52)

Instructions: Use the musical symbols to reveal each hidden message.

Expanded Activity: Identify each musical symbol. Give its name and briefly describe what it tells the musician.

41. HIDDEN WORD SEARCH

Age:	Older Elementary
Concept:	Hymn study
Use:	Follow-up to study of "Fairest Lord Jesus"
Materials:	Pencils, worksheet #41 (p. 53)

Instructions: Look for the hidden words from the hymn "Fairest Lord Jesus." Circle each word as it is located. Words may read up, down, across, backward, or diagonally. Write

the words you find in the correct stanza box.
Expanded Activity: Sing the hymn. This activity may be combined with the Hymn Page Worksheet (#19).

42. NOW THANK WE ALL OUR GOD

Age:	Elementary
Concept:	Hymn study
Use:	Introduction or follow-up to study of "Now Thank We All Our God"
Materials:	Hymnals, colored markers or pencils, worksheet #42 (p. 54)

Instructions: Read the story about this hymn. Complete the questions below. Color the picture.
Expanded Activity: Sing this hymn.

43. WORD SCRAMBLE

Age:	Elementary
Concept:	Hymn study
Use:	Introduction or follow-up to "Joyful, Joyful, We Adore Thee"
Materials:	Pencils and/or crayons, colored pencils, or markers, worksheet #43 (p. 55)

Instructions: Color in each block containing a numeral. The remaining letters spell words from a hymn. Write the words on the bottom of the sheet. See Answer Key on inside back cover.
Expanded Activity: Sing the hymn, "Joyful, Joyful, We Adore Thee." This activity may be combined with the Hymn Page Worksheet (#19) if you are teaching this hymn.

44. DOXOLOGY WORD SCRAMBLE

Age:	Elementary
Concept:	Doxology text
Use:	Study of the Doxology and its place in worship
Materials:	Pencils, worksheet #44 (p. 56)

Instructions: Unscramble each word to discover the text of the doxology. See Answer Key on inside back cover.
Expanded Activity: Sing the doxology setting most common to your congregation. Locate this setting in your hymnal. Look through the hymnal for additional settings of this text. Have a pianist play each setting and discuss how they are similar or different. Discuss where the doxology occurs in your worship service. Lead the children in a discussion of what this text means. This activity may be combined with the Hymn Page Worksheet (#19).

45. SCRIPTURE SEARCH: THE GOD OF ABRAHAM PRAISE

Age:	Older Elementary
Concept:	Hymn study and scripture references
Use:	Hymn study of "The God of Abraham Praise"
Materials:	Pencils, Bible, worksheet #45 (p. 57)

Instructions: Read each scripture reference. Select a phrase in the right column that best relates to the scripture. Write the corresponding number in the blank beside the scripture.
Expanded Activity: Sing the hymn. This activity may be combined with the Hymn Page Worksheet (#19).

46. FALL LEAF MATCH

Age:	Elementary
Concept:	Rhythm
Use:	Identify rhythmic values using various notes
Materials:	Pencils, worksheet #46 (p. 58)

Instructions: Draw a line from each leaf in the left column to a leaf in the right column that has the same number of beats. There may be more than one possible correct answer.
Expanded Activity: Create new rhythm patterns by combining several leaves. Have a volunteer point to leaves in random order as the children clap each pattern. Locate similar rhythm patterns in the music you are currently rehearsing.

47. LORD OF THE DANCE

Age:	Older Elementary
Concept:	Hymn study
Use:	Follow-up to study of "Lord of the Dance"
Materials:	Pencils (hymnal, if needed), worksheet #47 (p. 59)

Instructions: Draw a line connecting each phrase in the left column with its matching phrase in the right column.
Expanded Activity: Have the children number the completed phrases in the order of their appearance in the hymn. Locate the hymn in your hymnal and sing.

48. THE ORGAN

Age:	Older Elementary
Concept:	Organ
Use:	Introduction to the organ as an instrument and your church organ
Materials:	Pencils, worksheet #48 (p. 60)

Instructions: Answer each question based on the organ in your church.

Expanded Activity: Invite your organist to the rehearsal. Ask this person to demonstrate the organ for the children. If any of your students are studying the piano, invite them to play a piece on the organ. If you have a pipe organ, open the chamber so the children can see the pipes and wind supply.

49. SUPER SINGER CROSSWORD PUZZLE

Age:	Older Elementary
Concept:	Singing habits
Use:	General review of good singing habits
Materials:	Pencils, worksheet #49 (p. 61)

Instructions: Use the clues to complete the crossword puzzle. See Answer Key on inside back cover.

Expanded Activity: This activity may be combined with the Singer's Rules Worksheet (#40).

50. WHAT'S MY TIME?

Age:	Older Elementary
Concept:	Time signature
Use:	Review of time signatures and counting
Materials:	Pencils, worksheet #50 (p. 62)

Instructions: Add bar lines to each line of music based on the given time signature. Clap and count each line using the time signature as a guide.

Expanded Activity: Place rhythm instruments in the activity area. Once the worksheet is complete, children may play each pattern on an instrument. Identify the time signatures in all music you are currently rehearsing.

51. ON A SCALE OF 1 TO 8

Age:	Older Elementary
Concept:	Scales
Use:	Follow-up of scale study; combine with study of hymn "Holy, Holy, Holy"
Materials:	Pencils, worksheet #51 (p. 63)

Instructions: Write the scale degrees or letter names in the blanks provided below each note. Sing the patterns when the worksheet is completed.

Expanded Activity: You may combine this activity with the Hymn Page Worksheet (#19) using "Holy, Holy, Holy." Identify the scale used in each anthem or song you are currently rehearsing. Write the scale on the board and sing it.

52. HYMNS ADD UP TO A PERFECT SCORE

Age:	Older Elementary
Concept:	Hymn study
Use:	Introduction or follow-up to study of "Holy, Holy, Holy"
Materials:	Pencils, hymnal, worksheet #52 (p. 64)

Instructions: Complete each question, writing your response in the blank provided. Add the numbers in the right column. Your answer should equal 100.

Expanded Activity: Sing this hymn. This activity may be combined with the Hymn Page Worksheet (#19).

Same and Different

2.

Bethlehem Maze

14

Music Symbols Search

Locate and circle each hidden musical symbol. Color the picture.

Hidden words:
D.C.
D.S.
a tempo
fine
dim.
rit.
mp
p
mf

4.

Coded Picture
Color the picture using the code.

rit = get gradually slower . . . . Red

♩ = a "long" note . . . . .Blue

♪ = a "short" note . . . . .Yellow

⊕ = coda . . . . .Brown

D.C. = go back to the beginning . . . . .Black

D.S. = go back to the sign . . . . .Orange

𝄋 = the "sign" . . . . .Green

16

COSMIC WORKSHEET

DRAW A LINE FROM EACH SPACESHIP TO ITS CORRECT LANDING
PORT: SPACE NOTES TO THE SPACE STATION AND LINE NOTES TO
THE LINE STATION.

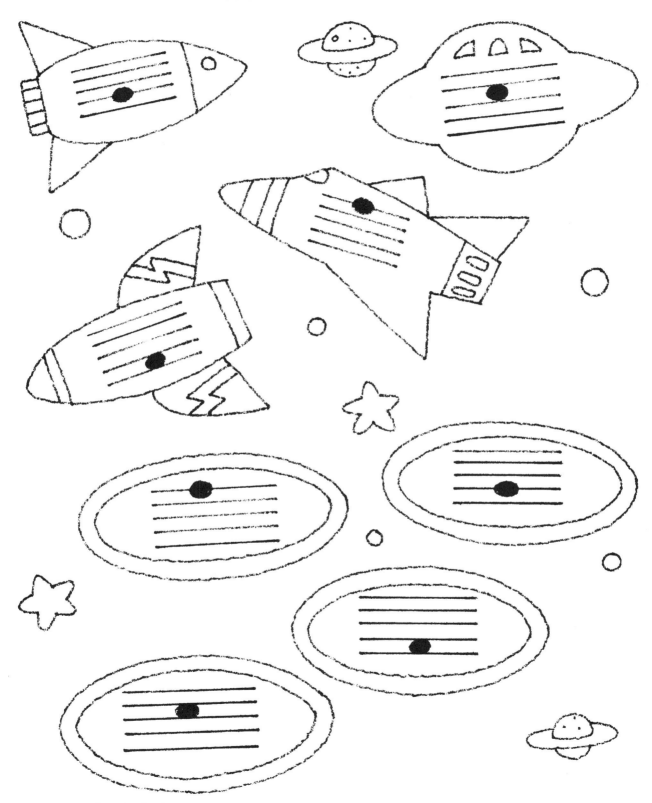

6.

Instrument Maze

Help the instruments praise God.
Find a path for each instrument to God. Color the picture.

A MUSICAL CHECKLIST

See how many different ways you use music.
Put an X in the box next to the ways you have used music.

❑ Sing in a church choir.

❑ Listen to the radio.

❑ Sing songs and hymns during worship services.

❑ Take piano lessons.

❑ Take instrument lessons.

   ❑ violin

   ❑ drums

   ❑ others_____

❑ Sing with family around the piano at home.

❑ Sing at school.

❑ Play tapes or CDs.

❑ Sing while on a trip in the car.

❑ Hum to yourself while doing chores.

❑ Whistle while walking down the street.

❑ Hear a band at a parade.

☼ **Write some other ways you enjoy music.**

8.

Fill in the blanks.

The name of my church is:

_____

My choir director is:

_____

My choir helpers are:

_____

_____

_____

My church organist is:

_____

My church pianist is:

_____

My church music director is:

_____

FOR GETTING ACQUAINTED

Try to find a different person to autograph each statement below.

2. I play on a ball team.

1. I have blue eyes.

3. I have an older brother.

4. I can play the piano.

5. My favorite subject in school is math.

6. I like to sing in choir.

8. I am in my school's band.

7. I like to eat hot dogs.

9. I like to talk on the phone.

10. I like Rocky Road ice cream.

11. I have an electronic keyboard at home.

12. I like to read.

14. I like to listen to music on the radio.

13. I have a younger sister.

15. I like to sleep late on Saturdays.

16. I will sing a solo in choir.

Balloon Rhythm Worksheet

Connect each child to the balloon that matches the shirt.

11. Rhythmic Language Worksheet

Did you know that music has a language all its own? Musicians around the world can look at a page of notes and hear what it will sound like.

Part of the language tells us about rhythms—how long a note will sound.

Can you translate these notes into their rhythmic language?
Write the correct letter below each note.

L = Long   S = Short

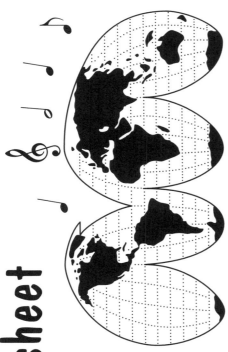

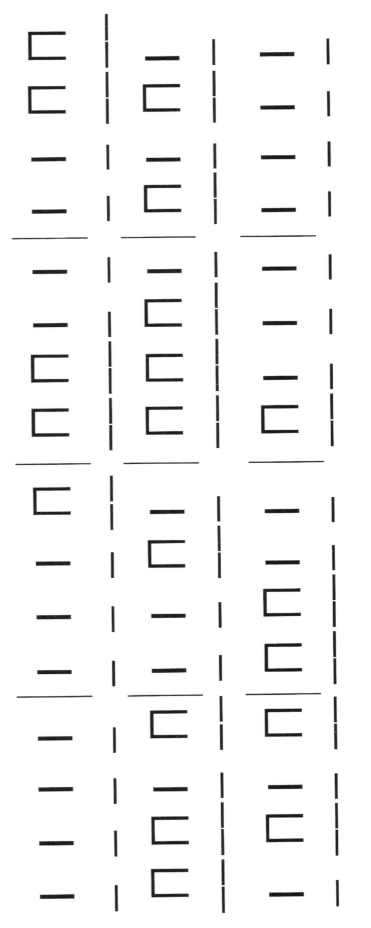

23

12. Melodic Movement GAME

These traveling notes are moving all around the staff.
Do the notes move by step, skip, or repeat? Show the
direction the notes move with an arrow ↓ ↑ or **R**.

Example:

Step ↑   **Skip ↓**   **Repeat R**

1.

2.

3.

4.

5.

6.

7.

8.

9.

10.

Where Is My Third?

Each note is written as a 5.
Can you write the third?
Remember: When 5 is on a line, 3 is on a line; when 5 is on a
space, 3 is on a space. Look at the example before you begin.

Example A:

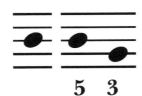

5   3

Example B:

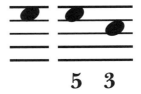

5   3

1.

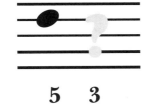

5   3

2.

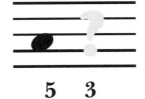

5   3

3.

5   3

4.

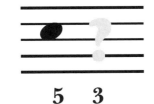

5   3

5.

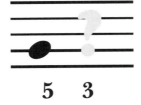

5   3

6.

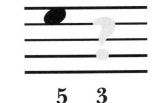

5   3

7.

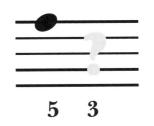

5   3

8.

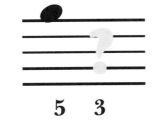

5   3

14. PSALM 23 WORD SEARCH

```
S H E P H E R D D S T
T A B L E E I N W V R
A Q R A F L G R E E N
F U I I J O H O L P Z
F O L L O W T D L A E
L I C O M F O R T T H
M L E A D S R B A H R
F S I G O O D N E S S
W A T E R S B Q R T H
```

**Find these words
in the sheep.
Search across,
up, down, and
diagonally.**

shepherd
green
waters
right
rod
staff
leads
table
follow
oil
paths
goodness
dwell
comfort
life

Psalm 23

The LORD is my shepherd, I shall
   not want.
 He makes me lie down in
   green pastures;
he leads me beside still waters;
 he restores my soul.
He leads me in right paths
 for his name's sake.

Even though I walk through the
   darkest valley,
 I fear no evil;
 for you are with me;
 your rod and your staff—
 they comfort me.

You prepare a table before me
 in the presence of my enemies;
you anoint my head with oil;
 my cup overflows.
Surely goodness and mercy
   shall follow me
 all the days of my life,
and I shall dwell in the house of
   the LORD
 my whole life long.

(NRSV)

Advent Hidden Word Puzzle

See if you can find the following words used in the Advent season. Search across, up, down, backward, and diagonally.

Advent
peace
prepare
waiting

shepherds
candles
prophets
angels
season

Messiah
manger
Christmas
welcoming

U	Y	S	T	R	E	W	Q	M	N	S	B
D	F	J	E	K	L	Z	X	C	P	D	V
S	A	P	O	L	E	R	A	P	E	R	P
J	Q	W	E	R	D	T	Y	W	U	E	I
R	I	S	H	T	G	N	U	E	F	H	V
S	Y	P	C	W	X	D	A	L	W	P	E
T	N	E	V	D	A	B	Z	C	A	E	I
E	G	A	T	H	S	I	I	O	R	H	O
H	U	C	H	R	I	S	T	M	A	S	P
P	F	E	R	V	E	W	E	I	D	A	A
O	A	Z	E	B	Y	S	C	N	N	X	S
R	R	O	M	G	P	S	L	Q	G	K	D
P	U	H	N	I	T	I	E	X	J	R	F
G	V	F	A	E	W	L	D	X	C	Y	J
A	Z	H	M	B	S	E	A	S	O	N	K

16.

Christmas
Word Search

See if you can find the following words used in the Christmas season.
Search up, down, across, backward, and diagonally.

Words to Find

Love	Precious	Room	Allelu
God	Hearts	Manger	Touch
Stories	Wrapped	Hope	Bare
Child	Joseph	Inn	Receive
Hands	Mary	Angels	
Star	Tired	Singing	

```
P  T  J  O  S  E  P  H  R  Q  N
M  O  S  K  T  P  A  M  F  C  F
A  U  P  S  A  L  L  E  L  U  T
R  C  G  V  R  T  I  R  E  D  C
Y  H  O  P  E  B  H  O  B  H  J
C  H  I  L  D  E  P  P  A  R  W
N  N  B  I  A  L  S  Z  R  P  X
D  U  E  R  M  A  N  G  E  R  E
S  Y  T  L  O  V  E  R  G  E  V
D  S  D  D  O  A  K  L  E  C  I
N  J  O  H  R  S  I  L  I  E  E
A  N  G  E  L  S  D  T  N  O  C
H  S  T  O  R  I  E  S  N  U  E
X  I  K  G  N  I  G  N  I  S  R
```

"I Sing a Song of the Saints of God" *Fill-in-the-Blanks*

17.

Fill in the missing words from this hymn. Choose words from the list below. Some words may be used more than once. When you have finished, check your work by finding this hymn in your hymnal.

I sing a _____ of the _____ of God, _____ and _____ and _____ , who toiled and _____ and lived and _____ for the _____ they _____ and knew. And one was a _____ , and one was a _____ and one was a _____ on the green; they were all of them _____ of God, and I mean, _____ helping, to be one too.

They _____ their Lord so _____ , so _____ , and his love made them _____ ; and they followed the _____ for _____ sake the whole of their _____ lives long. And one was a _____ , and one was a _____ , and one was _____ by a fierce wild _____ ; and there's not any _____ , no, not the _____ , why _____ shouldn't be one _____ .

They _____ not only in _____ past; there are _____ of thousands still. The _____ is _____ with the joyous _____ who love to do _____ will. You can meet them in _____ , on the _____ , in the _____ , in _____, by the _____ , in the _____ next door; they are _____ of God, whether _____ or _____ , and I mean to be one too.

Word List

hundreds	song	too	sea	beast	patient	dear
reason	slain	Lord	lived	Jesus'	strong	God
died	store	soldier	right	world	bright	queen
loved	least	school	brave	poor	true	
church	saints	priest	rich	ages	shepherdess	
good	I	doctor	house	fought	street	

18. # ONCE IN ROYAL DAVID'S CITY
Fill-in-the-Blank

Fill in the blanks with the missing words from the hymn. Choose words from the list below.
Some words may be used more than once. Color the picture.

Once in _____ David's city _____ a lowly _____ shed,

where a_____ laid her _____ in a _____ for his _____ ;

Mary, loving _____ mild, Jesus _____ , her little _____ .

He _____ down to _____ from heaven who is

_____ and Lord of _____ ,

and his _____ was a stable, and his _____ was a stall.

With the poor, the _____ ,

the lowly lived on _____ our _____ holy.

_____ is our childhood's pattern; _____ by _____ like us

he _____ ;

he was _____ , weak, and _____ , tears and _____

like us he knew;

and he feeleth for our _____ ,

and he _____ in our _____ .

Word List

mother	royal	manger	shelter
Christ	child	Jesus	shareth
gladness	Savior	cattle	cradle
bed	grew	smiles	
earth	sadness	day	
all	helpless	little	
God	came	baby	
scorned	stood		

30

Hymn Page Worksheet

Locate this hymn by using the indexes in your hymnal. Complete the following questions about the hymn page as a guide.

Hymn Title

_____

What is the hymn page number? _____

What is the subject? _____

Who is the composer? _____

What is the tune name? _____

What date was the tune composed? _____

What is the meter of the hymn? _____

Who is the author? _____

When were the words written? _____

What does this hymn text means to me? _____

_____

_____

_____

_____

20.

My Hymnal Worksheet

What is in your church hymnal? Many wonderful things are inside a hymn book. See if you can find these.

1. Hymn Title Index _____ (page)

2. Table of Contents _____ (page)

3. "All Glory, Laud, and Honor" _____ (page)

    Who wrote the words? _____ (page)

    Who wrote the music? _____ (page)

4. The Lord's Prayer _____ (page)

5. An order of worship _____ (page)

    What is this service? _____ (page)

6. Psalms (Responsive Readings) _____ (page)

7. "Tell Me the Stories of Jesus" _____ (page)

    When was the music written? _____ (year)

    On what scripture passages are the words

    based? _____

My #1 Choice

The hymn I like most Is:

Title: _____

Author: _____

Composer:

_____

Name of the hymn tune:

_____

Why this is my favorite hymn:

_____

_____

_____

Some favorite hymns of our congregation:

1. _____

2. _____

3. _____

4. _____

22.

"Come, Christians, Join to Sing!"

Word Search
Find the words from the list
in the puzzle below.
They may be up, down,
across, diagonal, or backward.

Go and
Search!

Christians
Amen
Heart
Sky
Love
Heaven

Sing
Praise
Guide
Voice
Lord
Goodness

Alleluia
King
Rejoice
Friend
Life

C	O	X	P	R	L	G	N	I	K
A	H	M	R	E	J	O	I	C	E
L	P	R	A	Q	L	A	R	I	J
L	L	M	I	A	M	E	N	D	G
E	O	E	S	S	I	N	G	Z	O
L	V	E	E	E	T	I	E	N	O
U	E	C	Y	F	R	I	E	N	D
I	E	I	T	I	A	E	A	P	N
A	R	O	Z	L	E	B	Y	N	E
N	E	V	A	E	H	V	L	K	S
Q	G	U	I	D	E	E	R	M	S

The Beatitudes Matching Activity

Matthew 5:1-11

Read Matthew 5:1-11 and match the column on the left with the correct response from the column on the right.

peacemakers

theirs is the kingdom of heaven

those who mourn

they will be comforted

merciful

they will see God

poor in spirit

they will be comforted

persecuted for
reighteousness' sake

they will be called
the children of God

hunger and thirst for
righteousness

they will inherit
the earth

meek

they will be filled

pure in heart

they will receive mercy

Things We Do In Choir

Use the secret code below to find out some things we do in choir.

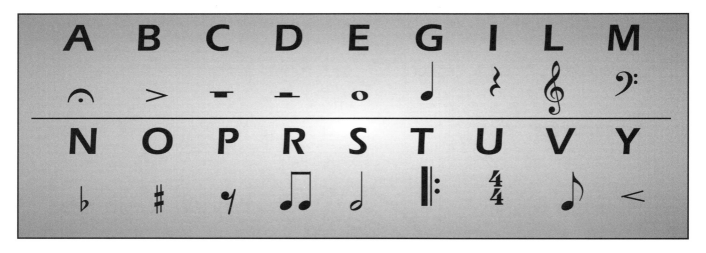

1.

2.

3.

4.

RHYTHM *Skeleton*

Write the correct letters below the rhythm symbols.

S = Short   L = Long   RL = Real Long   RRL = Real Real Long

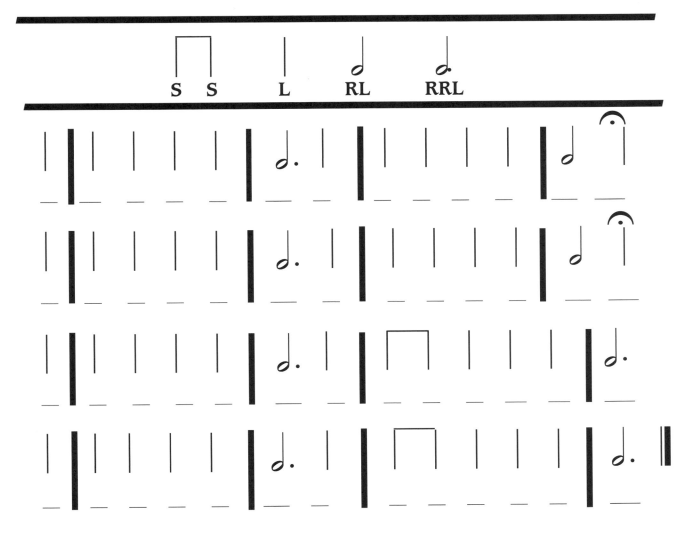

| S | S | L | RL | RRL |

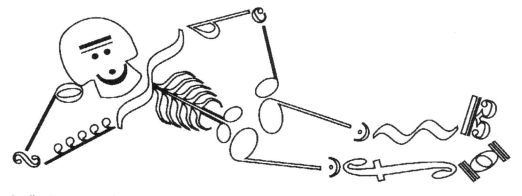

26.

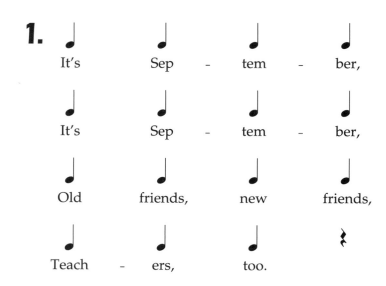

1.

It's Sep - tem - ber,

It's Sep - tem - ber,

Old friends, new friends,

Teach - ers, too.

SEPTEMBER:
A Fun Time of Year

Learn this fall round by reading aloud in the rhythm shown by the notes above each word.
Be sure to use your most expressive voice as you speak in rhythm.
To perform as a round:
1. The first group will read stanza 1.
2. Then the second group begins reading stanza 1 as the first group continues with stanza 2.
3. Finally, the third group begins stanza 1 as the first and second groups continue with the next stanzas.

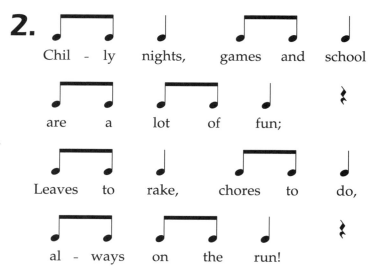

2.

Chil - ly nights, games and school

are a lot of fun;

Leaves to rake, chores to do,

al - ways on the run!

3.

It's a fun time of the year.

I am hap - py to be here.

It's Sep - tem - ber, hear my cheer,

Sing - ing, Sing - ing through the year!

Scripture Match

"Were You There"

Look up the following
Scripture verses and draw a line
to the appropriate phrase of
"Were You There."

crucified my Lord?   John 19:31-37

pierced him in the side?   Luke 23:44-49

sun refused to shine?   Mark 15:42-47

laid him in the tomb?   Matthew 27:32-37

Name the Note

Circle the notes below that you can find in the hymn.

Saints Hidden Message

Fill in the correct letters.
Who are these people? Put the correct letter in place by using the secret code.

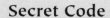

Secret Code

A	B	C	D	E	F	G	H	I	J	K	L	M	N	O	P	Q	R	S	T	U	V	W	X	Y	Z
5	19	8	11	18	2	22	15	6	13	10	14	24	1	21	25	12	7	26	3	17	23	20	9	4	16

1. __ __ __ __ __ __
   11 21 8 3 21 7

2. __ __ __ __ __
   12 17 18 18 1

3. __ __ __ __ __ __ __ __ __ __ __
   26 15 18 25 15 18 7 11 18 26 26

4. __ __ __ __ __ __ __
   26 21 14 11 6 18 7

5. __ __ __ __ __ __
   25 7 6 18 26 3

6. __ __ __ __ __ __ __ __ __ __ __
   21 1 18 20 5 26 26 14 5 6 1

Now, write the shaded letters above in the boxes below.

Next, unscramble these letters to solve the mystery of who these people are!

f G

"For the Beauty of the Earth"
Scale Step Worksheet

Fill in the blanks to tell how the notes move!

Up, down, or same? _____ _____ _____

Step, skip, or repeat? _____ _____ _____

5 ~ 3 ~ 1 Worksheet

5 is given in each example.
Write the 3 and the 1 below the given pitch.

Example

1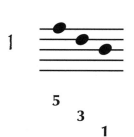

5
   3
      1

2

5
   3
      1

3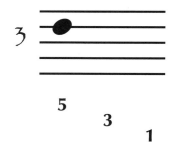

5
   3
      1

4

5
   3
      1

5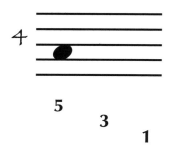

5
   3
      1

6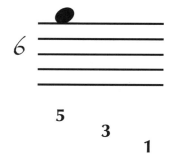

5
   3
      1

7

5
   3
      1

8

5
   3
      1

9

5
   3
      1

ANTHEM CLUES ^{31.}

Look at the entire piece of music for clues that will help you answer the questions below. Write your response in the space provided.

Song Title:_____

1. What is the tempo of this piece?

2. What dynamics are used in this piece?

3. What is the time signature of this piece?

4. How many different sections are in this piece? Where does each section begin?

5. How many quarter rests are in this piece?

6. How many accidentals (♯ ♭ ♮) are in this piece?

7. Do any notes have special symbols? (⌢ >).

Draw each symbol and write its location in the music.

8. Does the music contain any special road map instructions?

‖: D.C. 𝄋 ⊕

Draw each symbol and write its location in the music.

32.

TEST YOUR SKILLS

We've been learning the names of notes on the staff, key signatures, time signatures, rhythms, and lots of musical terms. You should be able to find your way through any song with very little trouble.
So, let's test your skill now.
Using your music, answer the questions below by writing down the correct measure in the song.
You may not find every item on the list.

1. Find the time signature.

2. Find the introduction.

3. Find the measure in which the choir begins to sing.

4. Find the first rest.

5. Find a term that tells you the tempo.

6. Find the key signature.

7. Find an accidental.

8. Find the first quarter note.

9. Find the dynamic marks.

10. Find the last measure of the music.

I'm Getting Longer!

Can you decode these rhythms into longer note values?
Write the note that is twice the value of the given rhythm.

Here's an example:

Now you try:

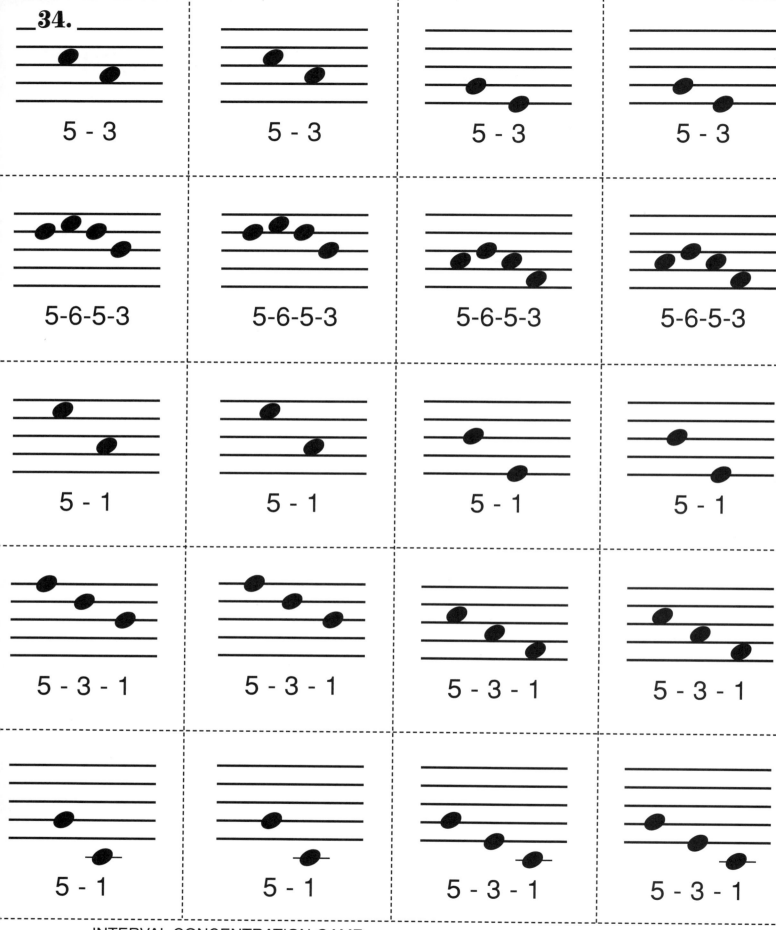

INTERVAL CONCENTRATION GAME
Duplicate on different colors of paper, laminate, and cut apart. Permission granted to duplicate.

RHYTHM *Adventure*

35.

Help these rhythms travel along. Write the correct rhythmic language below each example.

KEY: ♩♩ Short Short (S S)   ♩ Real Long (RL)   𝄽 Long (L)

♩ Long (L)   ♩ Real Real Long (RRL)   ▬ Real Long (RL)

EXAMPLE:
L L S S L

1. ♩ ♩ ♩ ♩

2. ♩ ♩ ♩

3. ♩ ♩.

4. ♩ ▬

5. ♩♩ ♩ ♩ ♩

6. ♩. ♩♩

7. ♩♩ ♩ ♩ ♩♩ ♩

8. ♩ ♩ ♩♩ ♩♩ ♩

9. ♩ ♩♩ ♩

10. ♩ ♩ ♩

11. ♩♩ ♩ ♩♩ ♩

12. 𝄽 ♩ 𝄽 ♩

13. ▬ ♩ ♩

14. ♩ ♩

15. ♩♩ 𝄽 ♩♩ 𝄽

16. ♩ 𝄽 𝄽

17. ♩ 𝄽

18. ♩ ♩ 𝄽 ♩

Permission granted to duplicate.

47

36. RHYTHM REVIEW

Fill in the blanks with the correct notes to create your own rhythm patterns.

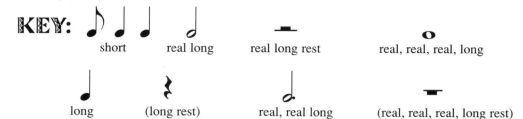

KEY: ♪ ♩ ♩   ♩   short   real long

―   real long rest

o   real, real, real, long

♩   long

𝄽   (long rest)

♩.   real, real long

▬   (real, real, real, long rest)

1. ___ ___ ___ ___ ___
long short short long long

7. ___ ___ ___ ___
long (long rest) long (long rest)

2. ___ ___ ___ ___ ___
long long long short short

8. ___ ___ ___ ___
short long short real long

3. ___ ___ ___
real, real long short short

9. ___ ___ ___ ___
long long long long

4. ___
real, real, real long

10. ___ ___ ___
long long (real long rest)

5. ___ ___ ___ ___ ___ ___ ___
short long short short short short short

11. ___
(real, real, real long rest)

6. ___ ___ ___
long real long long

12. ___ ___ ___ ___ ___ ___
short short long short short (long rest)

Ten Commandments of Singing

I. You shall be glad to share your talents and your learnings with others.

II. You shall know your music well before performing.

III. You shall watch your director at all times.

IV. You shall use good posture and take deep breaths.

V. You shall relax your jaw and lift your soft palate.

VI. You shall use your lips, teeth, and tongue to add consonants to the words that you sing.

(Add your own.)

VII.

VIII.

IX.

X.

38.

My Favorite Hymns

If you could choose the hymns for worship each week, what would they be?
There are different types of hymns needed for the different parts of a worship service.
Locate the Index of Topics and Categories in your hymnal and choose
your two favorites in the following categories.

1. The opening of a worship service—Choose hymns that express praise to God.

No./Title_____

No./Title_____

2. Responses—Choose hymns that can be a response to scripture or prayer.
Usually only a portion of a hymn is used as a litany response.

No./Title_____

No./Title_____

3. Invitation and commitment—Choose hymns that call people to make a commitment
to Jesus as Savior. Invitation hymns are usually sung at the end of a worship service.

No./Title_____

No./Title_____

4. Communion/Lord's Supper—Choose hymns that tell about the Last Supper
and Christ's Crucifixion.

No./Title_____

No./Title_____

5. Christmas—Choose hymns that are Christmas carols and tell about Jesus' birth.

No./Title_____

No./Title_____

6. Easter—Choose hymns that celebrate the Resurrection of Christ.

No./Title_____

No./Title_____

Crack the Code!

Text Decoder

Decode each line using the code below.

39.

Code:

A	B	C	D	E	F	G	H	I	J	K	L	M	N	O	P	Q	R	S	T	U	V	W	X	Y	Z
24	6	17	10	1	22	13	8	25	20	4	23	12	15	26	7	19	21	2	5	11	18	14	16	3	9

__ __   __ __ __ __ __ __ __ __   __ __ __ __ __   __ __ __ __   __ __ __ ,   __ __ __ __   __ __ __ .
14 1   17 8 25 23 10 21 1 15   7 21 24 25 2 1   3 26 11 21   3 26 11,   7 21 24 25 2 1   3 26 11.

__ __ __   __ __ __   __ __ __ __ __   __ __ __   __ __   __ __ __ __ __ __ __ __ .
13 26 10   14 8 26   23 26 18 1 2   24 23 23   17 8   25 23 10 21 1 15.

__ __   __ __ __ __ __ __ __ __   __ __ __ __ __   __ __ __ __   __ __ __ ,   __ __ __ __   __ __ __ .
14 1   17 8 25 23 10 21 1 15   7 21 24 25 2 1   3 26 11 21   3 26 11,   7 21 24 25 2 1   3 26 11.

__ __ __   __ __   __ __ __ __ __   __ __ __   __ __ __ __ __ __ 13!
13 26 10   2 26   13 26 26 10   24 15 10   23 26 18 25 15 15 13!

__ __   __ __ __ __ __ __ __ __   __ __ __ __ __   __ __ __ __   __ __ __ ,   __ __ __ __   __ __ __ .
14 1   17 8 25 23 10 21 1 15   7 21 24 25 2 1   3 26 11 21   3 26 11,   7 21 24 25 2 1   3 26 11.

__ __ __ __ __ __   __ __ __   __ __ __   __ __ __ .
7 21 24 25 2 1   3 26 11   1 18 1 21 3   10 24 3.

40. SINGER'S Rules

As you prepare for your worship service, remember that singers have very important rules for performing. Decode the rules below to help remind you how to be a Super Singer!

𝄢 = a	= b	= c	o = d	𝄞 = e	= g	= h
> = i	= k	= l	= m	# = n	= o	< = p
♭ = r	= s	= t	♮ = u	= v	= w	𝄋 = y

❶ _

❷ _ _ _ _ _ _ _ _ _ _ _ _ _ _ _ _ _

❸ _ _ _ _ _ _ _ _ _ _

❹ _ _ _ _ _ _ _ _ _ _ _ _

❺ _ _ _ _ _ _ _ _ _ _ _ _ _ _ _ _

❻ _ _ _ _ _ _ _ _ _ _ _ _ _ _ _ _ _

❼ _ _ _ _ _ _ _

❽ _ _ _ _ _ _ _ _ _ _ _

❾ _ _ _ _ _ _ _ _ _ _ _ _ _ _ _ _ _

52

Look for hidden words from the hymn "Fairest Lord Jesus." As you search up, down, across, backward, and diagonally, circle the words, then write them in the correct stanza box. Use this to help you sing the hymn from memory.

T	S	A	V	I	O	R	L	E	U	C	S
G	O	D	E	R	U	T	A	N	A	M	P
A	N	O	D	C	L	R	S	T	D	E	R
P	U	R	E	R	J	B	G	H	S	A	I
E	O	A	W	O	O	D	L	A	N	D	N
L	R	T	S	W	Y	E	I	N	C	O	G
A	E	I	M	N	S	O	E	G	H	W	L
J	L	O	G	U	P	S	H	E	O	S	O
S	U	N	S	H	I	N	E	L	S	I	R
C	R	E	F	A	I	R	E	S	T	N	Y
P	J	B	R	I	G	H	T	E	R	G	N
A	E	P	T	H	G	I	L	N	O	O	M

WORD LIST

ruler	praise	adoration	joy	savior
Jesus	sing	moonlight	brighter	crown
God	man	spring	Son	host
sunshine	woodland	Lord	purer	fairest
angels	glory	nature	meadows	

STANZA 1	STANZA 2	STANZA 3	STANZA 4

42.

Now Thank We All Our God

Martin Rinkart, born in 1586 in Eilenberg, Germany, was a German pastor. He not only loved preaching but he also loved music and singing. He even served as a choir boy while attending school in Leipzig. It was only natural that Pastor Rinkart would use his music as a source of strength and encouragement during a time of great difficulty and tragedy.

From 1618 to 1648, Pastor Rinkart and the people of Eilenberg were forced to endure the hardships of the Thirty Years' War. During this time there was not enough food to feed all the people who came to Eilenberg looking for a safe place to stay. As a result, there was much suffering and many people died. Pastor Rinkart conducted over 4,500 funerals, sometimes as many as forty or fifty in one day.

It was in the middle of this suffering and death that Martin Rinkart wrote the text of "Now Thank We All Our God." He intended it to be sung as a table grace before meals. Stanza 1 is his expression of thanksgiving for God's blessing, even during a time of war. Stanza 2 is a prayer for God's care. Stanza 3 is a doxology, praising God the Father, God the Son, and God the Holy Spirit.

Store the Facts

1. "Now Thank We All Our God" is found on page _____ in my hymnal.

2. _____ _____ wrote the text to be sung as a _____ _____.

3. The name of the hymn tune of "Now Thank We All Our God" is _____ _____.

4. The music was composed by _____ _____ and _____ _____.

5. Name another hymn that Felix Mendelssohn composed. _____

6. Stanza 1 is the author's expression of _____ for God's blessings.

7. Stanza 2 is a _____ for God's care.

8. Stanza 3 is a _____.

9. Name another hymn that is a doxology. _____

43.

Word Scramble

Find the words to a hymn in the chart below.
Color in each block with a numeral.
Write the words you find on the lines below.

3	2	J	6	O	8	Y	7	F	4	U	3	L	2	3	7	J	2	O	9	Y	5	F	7	6	U	4	L	3	6
5	8	7	3	E	9	7	4	9	A	4	D	9	3	5	O	6	R	7	E	9	6	2	7	8	8	E	8	4	E
3	4	G	7	O	9	D	8	7	5	O	2	F	9	3	G	L	7	O	9	R	3	Y	L	8	O	2	R	D	3
O	7	2	7	L	7	O	7	3	O	4	V	E	6	9	H	2	5	E	7	A	R	4	2	T	6	8	7	6	9
7	U	2	N	F	7	O	7	L	5	8	D	4	L	9	I	2	K	3	E	3	5	E	5	6	W	8	E	R	S
B	8	7	E	3	F	7	9	2	8	R	2	E	7	5	H	6	E	7	E	9	O	4	P	7	E	N	O	I	G
3	T	4	7	O	9	T	8	H	5	2	E	8	2	S	U	4	N	6	A	9	3	B	7	O	8	V	2	2	3

I found these words: _____

Doxology
Word Scramble

REIPAS ODG MFOR OWMH LAL SGIBNSLES WOLF;

_____ ___ ____ _____ ___ _____ _____;

REIPAS MHI LAL ARTECERUS RHEE WELBO;

_____ ___ ___ _____ ____ _____;

REIPAS MHI BVEAO EY VALEYNEH SOTH;

_____ ___ ____ ___ _____ ____;

REIPAS ETAHRF, ONS NDA OLYH OGTSH. MENA.

_____ _____, ___ ___ _____ _____. ____.

Scripture Search

"The God of Abraham Praise"

____a. Daniel 7:9   1. milk and honey (stanza 3)

____b. Exodus 3:14   2. Ancient of Everlasting
                              Days (stanza 1)

____c. Isaiah 40:31   3. Holy, holy, holy (stanza 4)

____d. Exodus 3:8   4. I Am (stanzas 1, 2, and 4)

____e. Deuteronomy 7:13   5. eagle wings (stanza 2)

____f. Genesis 3:22   6. tree of life (stanza 3)

____g. Isaiah 6:3   7. oil and wine abound
                              (stanza 3)

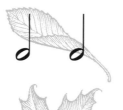

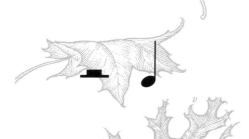

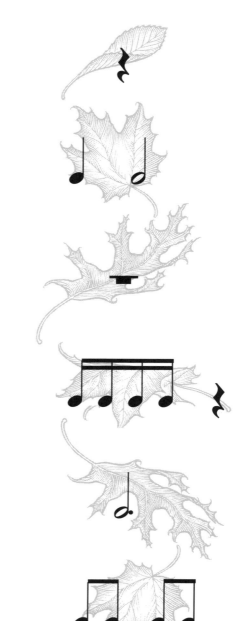

Fall Leaf Match

Draw a line from each leaf in the left column to a leaf in the right column that has the same number of beats. Some of the leaves in the left column match more than one leaf in the right column.

Key: ♩ = 1 beat   𝄽 = 1 beat   𝅗𝅥. = 3 beats

♫ = 1 beat   ♩ = 2 beats   𝅝 = 4 beats

♬ = 1 beat   ▬ = 2 beats   ▬ = 4 beats

"Lord of the Dance"

I danced on the sabbath	I had my birth
They cut me down	and the dance went on.
the holy people	and they hung me high;
but they would not dance	said it was a shame;
I am the Lord of the Dance	when the world was begun,
At Bethlehem	said he.
I danced on a Friday	with the devil on your back;
they came to me	and I still go on.
but I am the dance	and the stars and the sun,
and I came down from heaven	if you'll live in me;
I danced in the morning	and they would not follow me;
I am the life	for James and John;
and I danced in the moon	that'll never, never die;
I danced for the scribe	when I cured the lame,
and they left me there	and I danced on the earth.
it's hard to dance	on a cross to die.
they whipped and they stripped	and the Pharisee,
I danced for the fishermen,	and I leapt up high,
I'll live in you	and they thought I'd gone,
they buried my body	and the sky turned black;

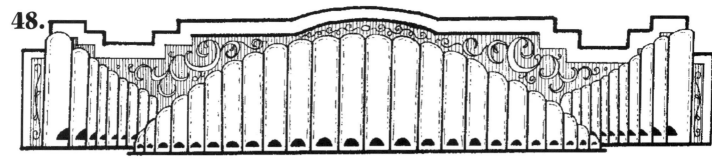

THE ORGAN

Can you think of an instrument that was invented a long time ago in Old Testament times? (Hint: it was first mentioned in Genesis 4:21, has become bigger and better, and is still being used in churches today.) It's an awesome instrument—the organ.

The sounds you hear from the organ are produced by blowing air through pipes. The pipes are **much** bigger than a pop bottle you might blow air into, so the air supply has to be powered by some other source than a person's lungs.

The Greeks developed the first organ about two hundred years before Christ was born. Their organ was powered by using water. Several hundred years later, the air pressure for the pipes was provided by bellows (a big box that takes in air and blows it out—the lungs of the organ). The smallest pipe organ has about 370 pipes, but the largest one has more than 40,000 pipes. A lot of air is needed!

Today, besides the pipe organ there is also an electronic organ that produces sounds electronically rather than sending air through pipes. The electronic organ is made to sound as much like a pipe organ as possible and is not as expensive as a pipe organ.

The part of the organ you see—the keyboard and controls—looks very much the same whether it is a pipe or electronic organ. Ask your church organist to show you these parts of the organ:

Manuals: Keyboards played with hands (most organs have two or three manuals, but can have as many as five or six).

Stops: Knobs or tabs used to control the kinds of sound the organ makes. There are four families of organ sounds: **Flutes, Strings, Foundations, and Reeds.**

Couplers: Knobs or tabs that connect keyboards or keys so that more than one keyboard sounds together.

Pedal-board: Keyboard played with the feet.

Swell pedal: Pedal that is moved by the feet; it controls the loudness or softness of the organ.

Crescendo pedal: Pedal that is moved by the feet to quickly add stops from softer to louder dynamic levels.

Pistons: Small buttons or toe studs (knobs pressed by the feet) to quickly change the organ's registration (stops that are used).

1. Does your church have a pipe organ or an electronic organ?

_____

2. How many manuals does it have? _____

3. Write the names of the manuals from top to bottom. _____

_____

4. Are the stops knobs or tabs? _____

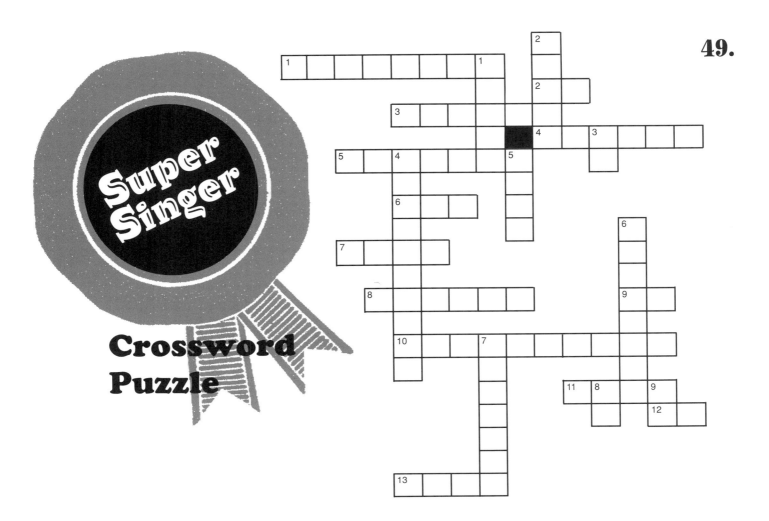

Across

1. How singers should sit or stand
2. The vowel sound for "give"
3. Word that describes A, E, I, O, U and sometimes Y
4. Sing _____to God
5. When you take in air to sing, you _____deeply
6. Watch the director for _____-offs
7. Stand _____and straight
8. When you sing in worship, you are a worship _____
9. The vowel sound for "end"
10. Alphabet letters that are not vowels
11. When you sing scripture, you are spreading God's _____
12. The vowel sound for "you"
13. Doing a good deed is sharing God's _____

Down

1. Open mouth and _____
2. Sing _____ (sharp) consonants
3. The vowel sound for the first syllable of "alleluia"
4. Always aim for _____ (the best)
5. Keep them on the director
6. Always watch the _____
7. Let your face _____when you sing
8. The vowel sound for "holy"
9. The name of the first note (home note) of the scale

50.

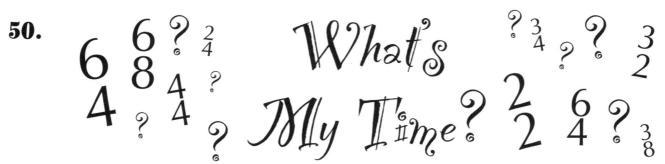

The **BOTTOM** number in a time signature tells us what kind of note gets the steady beat. If a 4 is on the bottom, a quarter note (♩) will get one beat. If a 2 is on the bottom, a half note (♩) will get one beat. If an 8 is on the bottom, an eighth note (♪) will get one beat. Study the chart below to understand the difference.

? 2	? 4	? 8
♩ = 1/2	♪ = 1/2	♪ = 1
♩ = 1	♩ = 1	♩ = 2
o = 2	♩ = 2	♩ = 4
	o = 4	o = 8

The **TOP** number in a time signature tells us how many beats should be in each measure. (A measure is the distance from one bar line (|) to the next.) Look at each line of rhythm below and add the bar lines. Be sure you look at the time signature carefully, first!

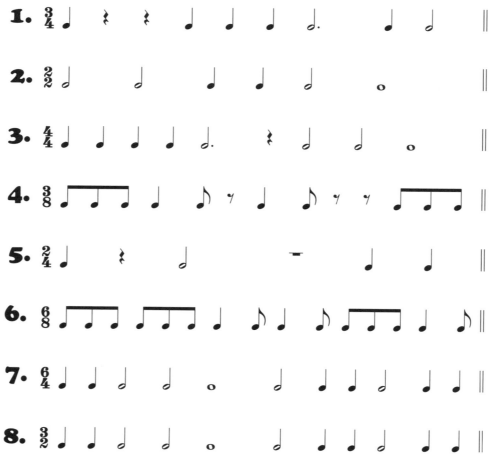

Note that lines 7 and 8 above (6/4 and 3/2) look alike. The notes can be in either time signature.

On a Scale of 1 to 8

Melodies are made up of tones found in scales. Scales usually have eight tones. Some musicians like to call each tone by its letter name. Some like to use numbers. And others like to call the tones by syllable names (*do, re, mi, fa, sol, la, ti, do*). Here are some little melody pieces for you to use for practice. Write the numbers or letters under the notes and then sing what you see.

C Major Scale

1 2 3 4 5 6 7 8
C D E F G A B C

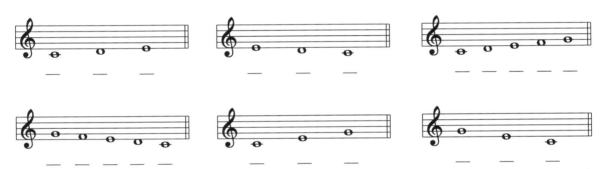

The melody of "Holy, Holy, Holy" is based on the tones of the D major scale. Look at the phrase below. The first note of the melody begins on scale number 1. In the blanks, write the number of the scale tones used in the melody. When you have finished, sing the melody using the numbers you have written.

D Major Scale

1 2 3 4 5 6 7 8
D E F# G A B C# D

52.

HYMNS ADD UP
To a Perfect Score

"Holy, Holy, Holy" is a great praise hymn sung by many types of churches. These words were written by Reginald Heber in 1826, the year he died at age forty-three. One year after his death, a collection of his fifty-seven choice hymns was published by his family and many friends. Most of these hymns are still in use today. "Holy, Holy, Holy" is a truly great hymn that praises God for who God was, is, and will be forever. That adds up to a **perfect score**.

Study the hymn in your hymnal to find the number that completes the statements or answers the questions below. Write the number in the blanks at the side.

1. How many measures are in the hymn?
   (A measure is from one bar to another: | |)   _____

2. How many letters are in the TUNE name?
   (The TUNE name is in capital letters.)   _____

3. How many measures contain only quarter notes? (♩)   _____

4. Fill in the blank: God in _____ persons.   _____

5. Find the measures in the melody line that have only whole notes. (𝅝)

   Multiply that number by the number of counts one
   whole note gets. _____ x _____ =   _____

6. How many counts are in each measure?
   (The top number of the time signature)   _____

7. Count how many times the world *holy* is used.
   Count how many times the word *Trinity* is used.
   Add the two totals.   _____

8. How many measures contain a half note? (♩)   _____

9. Read the entire hymn and add 32 to your total.   _____

Add the numbers down the right side of the page.
Is your total a perfect 100?   TOTAL =   _____